Becoming

the
Modern Proverbs 31
Woman

A 31-Day devotional through the Book of Proverbs

by Chrystal V. Bernard

For information about individual or bulk purchases, please contact Chrystal Bernard at **chrystal.v.bernard@gmail.com**.

ISBN 978-1-7344823-0-0 (paperback edition)
ISBN 978-1-7344823-1-7 (digital edition)

Unless otherwise indicated, all Scripture quotations are taken from the New King James Version of the Bible.

Dedication

This book is dedicated to Jesus Christ, who, during the course of writing this book, has challenged, pushed, and stretched my faith with grace and mercy. Thank you Lord for giving me a life I could have never dreamed of. You continue to pursue me, and I am eternally grateful for your loving kindness. I dedicate my entire being and life to your will, exchanging my desires for your desires to enhance your kingdom on earth.

I graciously accept the calling to encourage women of all ages to pursue YOU with excellence!

With Love,

Your Daughter, Chrystal

Acknowledgements

Sincere gratitude to my husband, children, mother and best friend, Jodi, for encouraging me through life to dig deep into the meaning of the Proverbs 31 woman.

Husband

Joshua Sr., your patience, encouragement and love has strengthened me to love God more than ever and pursue my God-given calling of entrepreneurship, ministry, motherhood and, of course, being your wife.

You saw the Proverbs 31 woman in me before I saw her in myself, and, for that, I am eternally grateful. Thank you for constantly leading and covering our family in prayer. I love you.

Children

Joshua Jr., Gabriella, and Londyn, you *all* are the best children for which a woman could ask. Thank you for allowing me to be your mom through the trials and errors of motherhood. Your child-like faith has taught me to love Christ in a fresh, genuine way.

Mother

Although I did not fully understand this until I was an adult, I have always had the example of a Proverbs 31 woman in my life. Thank you for living your life as a Proverbs 31 woman. Thank you, also, for encouraging and cheering me on beyond my comfort zone.

I am eternally grateful for our mother-daughter bond. I promise to one day put up the Christmas lights and decorations as you taught me when I was a child.

Best Friend

Jodi, your testimony of tribulation, hope and restoration changed my life and pushed my faith to a deeper level. God had a lifelong purpose for our sisterhood even in our "Before Christ" (B.C.) days! I am encouraged by you and your family, and I thank you for being a faith-filled woman and supporting me through the years.

You are a friend who has always been there, and I am forever grateful!

The Proverbs 31 Woman Club

Thank you readers for supporting the idea to gather women from all walks of life to fellowship together as we pursue God in excellence. Thank you for your virtual comments and encouragement. They inspired me to create this book.

Table of Contents

Introduction

After reading about the Proverbs 31 woman in the *Bible*, have you ever thought "Wow! She is a dynamic superwoman."? Upon an initial read, she does appear to be *the* perfect example, and just too far out of reach to actually embody. This 31 day devotional will demystify the Proverbs woman and what her characteristics look like in modern day.

The primary role of women living in the 21st century has shifted from homemaker exclusively to women who are not only wives and mothers but also leaders, business women, entrepreneurs, students, and athletes. Despite the shift in roles, the attributes of the Proverbs 31 woman have not changed but are enhanced all the more so to encompass technological advances, women's presence in the workforce, and the efficiency required in our fast paced society.

This devotion will define the Proverbs 31 woman and will enable you to address the changes and challenges of the modern world, and meet the needs of your family using the wisdom of the Lord as your guide. The devotional provides practical application steps for implementing the Lord's wisdom and questions to ponder, so you can hit the ground running on day one.

You were created by the Lord as His masterpiece. Reading this devotion will ensure spiritual chiseling, shedding off what was never intended for you by God, and becoming who God has called you to be. Instead of retreating from His pull on your life, submit and soar. The walk with Christ is an amazing, lifelong journey. He is ready to meet you with open arms as you surrender to him daily.

You will never be the same.

Book Structure

Proverbs Study

What is a devotional without the study of the *Bible*, God's perfect guide book and precious love letter to us? The book of Proverbs, specifically, is filled with the wisdom and information we must apply to become the Proverbs 31 woman. Grab a journal, pen, and coffee or tea as you dive into the word of God.

Read one chapter of Proverbs each day and one chapter in this devotional each day to complete this study and God's Word on the subject.

Devotion

Each devotion is inspired by the Holy Spirit to provide revelation and insight into the attributes and character of the Proverbs 31 woman, the best that God created us to be. Often, however, the Proverbs woman within us must be resurrected. We must tear off the frames that restrict us and the worldly ideologies that may hinder to fully recognize that woman within.

Read each devotional at the start of your day, and be open to the encouragement and the correction by the Holy Spirit.

Faith in Application

Ever wonder how to actually apply the revelation and wisdom of the Lord? The "Faith in Application" section in each chapter teaches practical steps for applying biblical instruction to life in the 21st century. The application steps are straightforward, and they are the connecting piece between wisdom and reality.

Questions to Ponder

The questions at the end of each chapter are to help you think through your life and how you can change your thoughts, actions and behaviors to reflect those of the Proverbs 31 woman. Be honest in your answers as truth and transparency is how you grow.

DEVOTIONS

Day 1, Chapter 1
Becoming a Daughter First

"and said, "Assuredly, I say to you, unless you are converted
and become as little children, you will by no means enter the
kingdom of heaven. Therefore whoever humbles himself as
this little child is the greatest in the kingdom of heaven."
Matthew 18:3-4

We are instructed to become like children and approach God as our true Father. Child-like faith and humility are determinants for entering the kingdom of God and ultimately the Lord's presence. We can enter God's presence through prayer, but often times, we approach Him with a checklist limited to our current needs and desires. Approaching prayer with this perspective is not only limiting, but also disallows experiencing the fullness of God's glory.

God desires more than our repetitive requests. He wants our heart, mind and spirit. He is delighted when we choose to partner with Him to accomplish His will and purposes for our lives. Our mindset during prayer should be one of surrender and partnership. Then we are truly walking with the Lord.

The goal is not just to receive blessings but to enjoy and experience God in his fullness and majesty. We can have that if we seek it. The veil has been lifted, and His presence is available to those who desire him.

Before we can be excellent women, wives, mothers, business women and students, we must first become daughters of our Lord. Become a daughter of the true Father and embrace His presence and glory in a childlike manner. Your prayer life will flourish as it is based on an eternal bond with the Father who loves us perfectly. This is not a relationship of obligation but one of preference, priority, and pure love.

Faith in Application

1. Carve out time for intentional prayer and relational time with the Lord. Spending time with the Lord at the beginning of the day helps renew and maintain focus on the Lord throughout the entire day.

2. Instead of focusing primarily on prayer petitions and requests, approach the Lord with an open heart and mind in expectation that He will surround you with His presence.

3. If easily distracted, leave your phone, computer or any other item that may lead you to lose focus on the Lord outside of your quiet space.

Questions to Ponder

1. The Proverbs 31 woman understands that she is a daughter first before the responsibilities of wife, mother, and career woman. How can you ensure that you begin each day with the understanding that you are a daughter of God before anything else?

2. How does this change your perspective and influence when

dealing with others, either within or outside of the home?

Day 2, Chapter 2
Wisdom, Instruction, and Self-Discipline

"An excellent woman [one who is spiritual, capable, intelligent, and virtuous], who is he who can find her? Her value is more precious than jewels, and her worth is far above rubies or pearls."
Proverbs 31:10 AMP

O ur flesh is weak however if we rely on God's strength and wisdom, we are assured that we can complete our calling with excellence. So, why is it difficult to do that at times? The mind knows what it must do, but the follow through is often the challenge and even the burden.

The first chapter of Proverbs addresses this issue. It tells us that our decision making and actions must be God ordained rather than flesh directed. Proverbs 1:7 explains how our wisdom is derived from the respectful fear of God, and our wisdom increases with instruction and self-discipline.

Wisdom
Instruction from God.

Instruction

Practical steps to accomplish.

Self-Discipline
Intentional choice to apply wisdom and instruction.

Though God's step-by-step instructions and wisdom are clear, our choice not to apply what we learn can be rooted in a lack of self-discipline or inconsistent application. As we embark on this 31 day challenge, I encourage you to ask the Lord to strengthen your level of discipline as you receive His wisdom and instruction. Self-discipline is crucial as the Lord may lay items on your heart to accomplish within this challenge. When wisdom is received, put the practical instruction into action and be disciplined to carry it out. This is the key to true obedience.

The 31st chapter of Proverbs begins with describing a virtuous woman as excellent and spiritual, making her more valuable than rubies and pearls. The chapter ends with praising her because she fears the Lord, reverently worshiping, obeying, serving, and trusting Him with awe-filled respect. She understands that her intimate relationship with God and the application of His wisdom is key in managing her household, having a successful marriage, and leading multiple business ventures. Wisdom is the connecting piece that allows us to partner with God in all that we do.

"Charm and grace are deceptive, and [superficial] beauty is vain, But a woman who fears the Lord [reverently worshiping, obeying, serving, and trusting Him with awe-filled respect], she shall be praised."
Proverbs 31:30 AMP

Faith in Application

1. Trust that God's wisdom is available for every situation and

can answer any need, even in the small things. Nothing is too great or too small for the Lord.

2. Write down the instructions received and hang them where you can read often (ie. on a mirror or a wall).

3. Ask the Lord to strengthen your level of discipline. Begin disciplining yourself in everyday tasks such as timeliness, exercise, food choices, household chores and even washing off makeup at the end of the day. This will help build the character of discipline and the daily diligence required for more significant instructions to come.

Questions to Ponder

1. How can you better ensure that you seek the Lord's wisdom and not rely on human understanding?

2. What routine tasks can you commit to becoming more disciplined? Practicing will build your overall discipline endurance.

Day 3, Chapter 3
Confidence & Security

"The heart of her husband safely trusts her; so
he will have no lack of gain. She does him good
and not evil all the days of her life."
Proverbs 31:11-12

W e can walk confidently and securely in our God given
purpose and excel in everything we do as daughters
of the King. We do not have to rely on applause from
others as our inner strength is rooted in our Father and Lord. This
divine assurance provides grace to care for the people closest to
us.

The self-confident nature of the Proverbs 31 woman enables
her to provide a safe place for her husband to trust his heart. Her
integrity, trustworthiness, and wise choice of words instill confidence in him to embark on the day and return home knowing she
has properly managed the affairs of the home - physically, mentally, and spiritually.

He can share his inner feelings with her and seek advice without fear of judgement. He can lead his home with confidence because his heart is protected. In short, she provides an atmosphere

of security and comfort not only for her husband and children, but for all the people connected to her.

The foolish woman, on the contrary, can harm her home financially, materially and emotionally. Instead of creating a safe haven for her family, she squanders her resources and creates a hostile environment that does not allow for trust and growth.

By following Godly wisdom and allowing ourselves to be led by the spirit, we can emulate the actions and character of the Proverbs 31 woman and provide a safe space for our loved ones. Ask the Lord how you can better create an atmosphere of trust, confidence, and security for the people closest to you.

Faith in Application

1. Become a good listener and fill your conversation with responses of interest and compassion.

2. Be present in your home. Put down the phone or any other distracting items that can take away from quality time spent with your husband or children.

3. Be mindful of your tone and demeanor to ensure your speech reflects understanding, patience, love, and respect.

Questions to Ponder

1. Whether you are single or married, how do you provide an atmosphere of confidence, security, and encouragement for the people closest to you?

2. What practical things can you put in place to ensure you speak the truth in love and provide unconditional love to those around you?

Day 4, Chapter 4
Producing vs. Procrastinating

"She seeks wool and flax, and willingly works with her hands."
Proverbs 31:13

T he Proverbs 31 woman is creative, resourceful, and hard working. Verse 13 highlights her eagerness and cheerful, willing attitude as she completes tasks. She strives always to be and do her best.

New endeavors and milestones, including marriage, childbirth and career advancement, are particularly exciting. We are eager to begin the associated tasks that come with these moments, but redundancy and time can shift the excitement into routine tasks, fading the initial zeal into obligation. We have to be on guard against becoming doers without excitement and gratitude for these blessings. The lack of eagerness and gratefulness not only affects productivity, but also fuels procrastination and discontent.

"Do not withhold good from those to whom it is due, When it is in the power of your hand to do so. Do not say to your neighbor, "Go, and come back, And tomorrow I will give it,"When you have it with you."" **Proverbs 3:27-28**

We are to carry out our God given responsibilities willingly and in a timely manner. This is part of what makes us "excellent women"! The Lord has provided us with the resources and abilities to complete our tasks efficiently and cheerfully. We should be seeking continually the Lord's plan for our life, His discernment about what tasks to take on, and His wisdom for what to do during the various seasons in our lives. If we allow God to lead, then we will not take on too much, do too little, or choose wrongly where to invest our efforts.

We must seek God's wisdom to complete the tasks with excellence that He has ordained for our lives. Proverbial women do not sit on the sidelines. Joyce Meyer once said that, "The best intentions do not produce results." Proverbial women are doers, helpers and producers. Ask the Lord to help you prioritize and complete tasks in a cheerful, eager and timely manner.

Faith in Application

1. Write down your responsibilities including child rearing, being a wife, working outside of the home, educational pursuits, church attendance, etc. Ask the Lord how you can prioritize your responsibilities and complete each task with a cheerful and willing heart.

2. Write down your secondary activities including volunteer work, parent/teacher organizations, youth sports involvement, etc. Ask the Lord if you have overcommitted on the secondary level at the expense of your primary responsibilities. We cannot have a heart of gratitude and a happy disposition as we fulfill our responsibilities if we feel overwhelmed and overburdened. Seek discernment and prioritize, so that you are doing not from obligation but with a cheerful heart.

Questions to Ponder

1. Are there any responsibilities you fulfill out of obligation? This can include raising your children, being a wife, completing educational pursuits, etc.

2. Are you quick to begin a task but procrastinate completing it? How can you better ensure you are in a state of willing production?

Day 5, Chapter 5
Like a Merchant Ship

"She is like the merchant ships loaded with foodstuffs;
She brings her household's food from a far [country]."
Proverbs 31:14 AMPC

I n biblical times, merchant ships were critical to commerce and trade, and even in sustaining life, particularly in foreign countries. They brought food and new spices, life-saving salves and oils, and exotic goods and fabrics that inhabitants were eager to purchase. The buyers in these foreign countries would either consume the products personally or resell them at market.

The Proverbs 31 woman is compared to this life sustaining vessel. She obtains the best for her family and at the best price. She is resourceful to not limit her family's needs to local stores and markets but seeks the best quality for her household's needs and budget from near and far.

Have you ever been to the home of a grandmother or mother whose pantry is stocked full? She readily has food available for her family and visitors and likely has items in her pantry that one has never seen before.

The Proverbs 31 woman understands that a carefully-stocked home creates comfort for the people around her, and adds a sense of security for the family members. She is always ready for an emergency or a need because she has anticipated it, purchased what was necessary, and knows what to do. Guided by the wisdom of the Lord as her compass, she steers her ship with care and confidence.

Faith in Application

1. Examine your pantry regularly to ensure your home is well stocked. No one wants to run out of toilet paper, or medicine for a burn, or a band aid for a scraped knee. Be prepared for every circumstance and your stress level will be diminished, and the safe haven you've created for those you love will be appreciated.

2. Try an online delivery service such as Instacart, which delivers groceries and household items from multiple stores for a low fee. You will save on time and gas costs, and avoid impulse buying. Just open an online cart and add to it when household items run low.

Questions to Ponder

1. How are you like a merchant ship? Assess how well you clean and stock your home. What changes should you make?

2. How can you ensure that you are not propelled by fear in stocking your home but by the Lord's wisdom?

Day 6, Chapter 6
Pure Intentions

"For the word of God is living and active, sharper
than any two-edged sword, piercing to the division of
soul and of spirit, of joints and of marrow, discerning
the thoughts and intentions of the heart."
Hebrews 4:12

Often we desire certain actions and results in our homes, but have the wrong intentions. How many times has a loved one left something on the floor and instead of picking it up or politely asking them to do so, our response was critical or our questions sarcastic? (i.e. "Do you see that sock on the floor?" "Are you going to wear that sock today?")

The questions may seem harmless, but they are really dishonest and manipulative. We need to be honest and direct with our loved ones. Our words reflect what's in our hearts. Are we seeking the Lord for how to speak to and treat others?

"Therefore whoever hears these sayings of Mine, and does them, I will liken him to a wise man who built his house on the rock:" **Matthew 7:24**

The Lord wants our intentions to match our words and actions. He wants our intentions to be pure and just. He examines our heart and thoughts for our motives and desires, and He convicts us when we are not encouraging, correcting and edifying from a heart of love. If we are truly trying to build strong and lasting homes and relationships, our intentions should be like those of the master builder; to build a firm foundation, to choose our tools wisely, and to execute each step with care.

The Proverbs 31 woman pursues the will of God in building foundations, edifies rather than condemns, and encourages rather than highlighting weaknesses. Her intentions are clear and her motives are pure. Her goal is to edify the people in her life with soothing words, a secure space and a comforting atmosphere.

Faith in Application

1. When in potential conflict, think about your reaction and response before speaking. If you feel you are going to respond harshly, over emotionally or with impure motives, hold your response until your heart is in the right place. Learning to hold your tongue is hard. Ask the Lord to help you in this area.

2. Ask yourself why you are responding from a particular perspective to a situation. Is it to get your way? To ridicule the other person? To elevate yourself? The key, even in conflict, is to remember that you are helping to shape the hearts and minds of others.

Questions to Ponder

1. How do you ensure pure intentions and avoid demeaning or

shameful speech when speaking?

2. Rather than just scratching the surface, how do you address the root and resolution of an issue with love and respect?

Day 7, Chapter 7
Review & Reflection

This week we learned that the Proverbs 31 woman is filled with wisdom, instruction, and self-disciple. Her respectful fear of the Lord is what drives her to not only hear from Him, but also to be disciplined enough to apply the wisdom obtained.

She knows she is the daughter of the King, that she is a producer rather than a procrastinator, an edifier rather than a criticizer, and that she designs and builds a safe, secure and well-stocked home. This is a woman we must emulate! Although becoming a Proverbs 31 woman may not happen overnight, the goal is to grow daily into her character.

Faith in Application

1. Take time to rest in the word of God. Review Proverbs 1-7 and the work you've completed in this devotional for the past seven days.

2. Expand the length of your quiet time to hear your next in-

struction from God. This may come as a quiet voice, a stirring in our spirit or a clear conviction.

Questions to Ponder

1. What qualities of the Proverbs 31 woman stood out from this past week's study? (Be sure to note them in a journal for future referencing.)

2. In what areas has the Lord encouraged you to grow? Did you take immediate action in that area? If so, what was the result?

Day 8, Chapter 8
Early Rising

"She rises also while it is still night and gives food to
her household and assigns tasks to her maids."
Proverbs 31:15 AMP

Have you ever risen late from the night's sleep, just when
everyone else in the house was getting up and demand-
ing your attention or, even worse, moments before you
must leave for a destination? Chaos and confusion is usually the
result, and you spend the day playing a game of catch up. It is as if
you and the day are in fierce competition for the upper hand.

The Proverbs 31 woman understands the wisdom and importance of rising early. This allows her day to be well-planned and
unrushed, encouraging her to linger in the Lord's presence before
familiar voices of the household fill the home.

Calm is the key to beginning her day. She is able to hear more
clearly of the wisdom of the Lord, including how to prioritize her
professional life, personal agenda, children's school obligations,
and the needs of her husband. Rising early is how she "dots the i's

and crosses the t's" to ensure the day flows smoothly and productively.

She goes a step further to divide the tasks she will take ownership of and the tasks she will outsource to others including helpers, caregivers, and other support systems (Hello Instacart!). Physical and mental exhaustion are prevented by simply planning and outsourcing, allowing the day to begin from a place of physical and mental rest. Using keen wisdom from the Lord, the Proverbs 31 woman prioritizes her day for the good of herself and household so that she will fulfill her responsibilities with grace and ease.

Faith in Application

1. Create a bedtime routine that is soothing and relaxing, and then discipline yourself to be in bed at least six to seven hours prior to your awakening.

2. Once up, go directly into your devotion time with the Lord. Grab coffee or tea and enjoy the time in his presence while your home is still quiet. This a great time to journal and study scripture as well.

Questions to Ponder

1. Are you an early riser? How can rising early help to establish authority and ease over your day?

2. What are practical things you need to put in place to ensure you can consistently rise early?

3. What is your new awakening time? _____

Day 9, Chapter 9
Wise Stewardship

"She considers a [new] field before she buys or accepts it
[expanding prudently and not courting neglect of her present
duties by assuming other duties]; with her savings [of time
and strength] she plants fruitful vines in her vineyard."
Proverbs 31:16 AMPC

T he Proverbs 31 woman is an excellent steward of her resources and her finances. She spends and invests wisely. If
she works outside the home as well, she does not do so just
so she can spend more and acquire more. With an eye to the future
for her family, she saves and invests thoughtfully and carefully.
The Lord speaks extensively about how to handle money, so seeking His wisdom before making any major decision is critical.

"Good planning and hard work lead to prosperity, but hasty
shortcuts lead to poverty." **Proverbs 21:5 NLT**

Although important, wise stewardship is more than creating
and sticking to a budget. It's about properly managing what you
have now, so that you might be entrusted with future increase.

The Lord's resources are unlimited, however He is careful about how much to entrust in us and bases that on how we handle what we already have. If we cannot be trusted to handle well $1,000, how can we be entrusted with $10,000?

"He who is faithful in what is least is faithful also in much; and he who is unjust in what is least is unjust also in much." **Luke 16:10**

The Proverbs 31 woman is prepared for increase. She knows the state of her accounts at all times, what she owns, who she owes, and she is fully aware of her family's financial forecast. She keeps careful records and is well-organized so her financial obligations are timely met and so that she can tithe to the Lord with a joyful heart.

"Be diligent to know the state of your flocks, and attend to your herds; " **Proverbs 27:23**

Faith in Application

1. If you do not manage your money, it will manage you. You must take charge, be responsible, and live within your means. Create a zero-based budget by writing down your income and expenses. Put money needed for your expenses in envelopes to ensure you pay what you must. If any money is left over, pay down any debt you may have, open a savings account, or invest.

2. Begin tithing. God asks that we trust Him for our care. One way to show we trust the Lord is to do as He asks and tithe 10% of our income. You will see great spiritual and financial blessings from your diligence.

"Bring all the tithes into the storehouse, that there may be food in My house, and try me now in this," says the Lord of hosts, "If I will not open for you the windows of heaven and pour out for you such a blessing that there will not be room enough to receive it." **Malachi 3:10**

Questions to Ponder

1. Would the Lord agree that you are a good steward of your finances? What practical changes can you make to ensure you are faithful with what He has already given you?

2. List the changes you will make in handling your finances. In what ways are you going to prepare for future increase?

Day 10, Chapter 10
An Attitude of Influence

"You are the salt of the earth. But if the salt loses its saltiness, how can it be made salty again? It is no longer good for anything, except to be thrown out and trampled underfoot.

"You are the light of the world. A town built on a hill cannot be hidden. Neither do people light a lamp and put it under a bowl. Instead they put it on its stand, and it gives light to everyone in the house.

In the same way, let your light shine before others, that they may see your good deeds and glorify your Father in heaven."
Matthew 5:13-16 NIV

The Proverbs 31 woman does not have to demand authority with her attitude, tone, or words. Her power to influence comes from her confidence in her God-given abilities and her relationship with the Lord Jesus Christ.

When she seeks the Lord, He empowers her. He gives her just the right words to express in just the right tone of voice. When she seeks the Lord, He emboldens her to speak with truth and confidence. When she seeks the Lord, He removes her doubt and fears, so she can move forward in her life and impact the lives of others. When she seeks the Lord, she is a force, with a soft demeanor.

Have you ever met another woman whose demeanor and disposition were so powerful that, even without speaking a word, she changes the course of your life? Her confidence and influence is obvious, and she sparks in you a desire to be different.

The Proverbs 31 woman is that person. Her attitude is one of hope and not despair, and people are attracted to her confident, unwavering faith. She's not interested in what the world dictates, but walks divinely in the lane God has set apart for her. She is not driven by the voices of man but by the still, quiet voice of the Lord. She is not strengthened by the accolades of society, but by the power imbued to her through depending on the Lord.

Unlike those who are driven by the world's values and views, the Proverbs 31 woman and God are on the same page. Changes in her are Holy Spirit driven, and when He moves, she moves. She has the power to positively impact the home, workplace and community for the glory of God. She can even influence a hostile world with her demeanor, disposition, and dedication to the Lord.

"in all things showing yourself to be a pattern of good works; in doctrine showing integrity, reverence, incorruptibility, sound speech that cannot be condemned, that one who is an opponent may be ashamed, having nothing evil to say of you." **Titus 2:7-8**

Faith in Application

1. Oftentimes, we end up worsening a situation we hoped to resolve. When you feel yourself wanting to respond in a worldly manner, take a step back, no matter how hard it is and

yield to the Holy Spirit. Anchor yourself in the Lord and what His word has to say about a particular situation.

2. Create a plan for how to handle difficult situations in a Godly manner and practice what you will say and how you will say it.

3. Pray for God to give you the words you need, and the attitude you need to reflect. Depend on Him.

4. Ask the people in your life to give you feedback about your overall attitude and demeanor. The responses may be humbling but honest feedback is how you grow.

Questions to Ponder

1. What steps will you take to maintain a Godly stance in a hostile environment?

2. How can you be more in tune to the prompting of the Holy Spirit, to ensure that when He moves you, you actually move?

Day 11, Chapter 11
Spiritual Endurance

"She equips herself with strength [spiritual, mental, and physical fitness for her God-given task] And makes her arms strong."
Proverbs 31:17 AMP

Womanhood ushers in the roles of business woman, wife, mother, student, sister, friend, and daughter. One can easily become overwhelmed with wearing those various hats and lose oneself in the midst of supporting others.

The Proverbs 31 woman is enabled for the tasks and roles portioned to her by quenching her daily spiritual thirst through the Lord who is her source of strength. When she is filled with His power, she is unstoppable, capable of functioning in all her roles at her optimum. She understands embracing the spirit of the Lord provides her an eternal, divine strength that does not run dry.

As women, we must prioritize our covenant with the Lord. He has equipped us with the mind of Christ to execute our life responsibilities effectively for the glory of God. Instead of reaching for the world system, we are to surrender daily with open arms to the Father who provides spiritual endurance to not only endure, but to succeed victoriously.

"On the last day, that great day of the feast, Jesus stood and cried out, saying, "If anyone thirsts, let him come to Me and drink. He who believes in Me, as the Scripture has said, out of his heart will flow rivers of living water." **John 7:37-38**

"Be anxious for nothing, but in everything by prayer and supplication, with thanksgiving, let your requests be made known to God;" **Philippians 4:6**

A Prayer for Spiritual Endurance

"For this reason I bow my knees to the Father of our Lord Jesus Christ, from whom the whole family in heaven and earth is named, that He would grant you, according to the riches of His glory, to be strengthened with might through His Spirit in the inner man, that Christ may dwell in your hearts through faith; that you, being rooted and grounded in love, may be able to comprehend with all the saints what is the width and length and depth and height — to know the love of Christ which passes knowledge; that you may be filled with all the fullness of God." **Ephesians 3:14-19**

Faith in Application

1. Surrender to God daily and allow the Holy Spirit to guide and direct your every move. He has promised to be by your side always, so seek His presence first before making that decision or phone call, writing that letter or email, declining that job or invitation. "Seek first the Kingdom of God and His righteousness and all things shall be added to you." What a promise!

2. Decide to emulate Christ in your every choice and behavior,

even when you don't feel like it.

3. When in prayer draw a line down the center of your journal. On the left side, write questions such as "What is the priority today?' or "What do I need to focus my energy on today?" On the right side, list God's responses. His impressions may be delivered through the Word or a devotion, as a quiet voice or spiritual impression or prompting. The key is getting quiet so you can discern correctly.

4. Remember, that God will never instruct you to do something contrary to the Bible.

Questions to Ponder

1. How will you discern if your responsibilities and roles are self or God ordained? Ask the Lord to identify roles and responsibilities you may have taken on that are not meant to be.

2. What steps are you going to take to seek spiritual strength, and to listen to the promptings of the Holy Spirit for your day, year and life?

Day 12, Chapter 12
Mental Strength

"She equips herself with strength [spiritual, mental, and physical
fitness for her God-given task] And makes her arms strong."
Proverbs 31:17 AMP

G od is equally concerned about our state of mind as He is
our actions and behaviors. To be truly excellent women,
we must take authority of our thoughts.

"For the weapons of our warfare *are* not carnal but mighty in
God for the pulling down of strongholds, casting down arguments
and every high thing that exalts itself against the knowledge of
God, bringing every thought into captivity to the obedience of
Christ," **2 Corinthians 10:4-5**

The slightest entertainment of a carnal thought can open a
port hole for the enemy to bring devastation. How many times
has a thought entered your mind and, before you knew it, if was
far from Godly? The mind, if not bridled and renewed, can be the
ruination of our lives, relationships, careers, and certainly our
testimony.

Though we become a new creation when we accept Jesus into our heart, our flesh is still at war with our faith. Our mind is often the enemy of our new heart. This is the true battleground for which we must be equipped.

"Guard your heart above all else, for it determines the course of your life." **Proverbs 4:23 NLT**

Meditating on, knowing, and applying the Word of God are the weapons of choice to be used for battle. Coupled with prayer and obedience, the Word perfectly aligns us with the will of God, renews our mind, and restores our hope to look heavenward and not at the world.

"For the word of God *is* living and powerful, and sharper than any two-edged sword, piercing even to the division of soul and spirit, and of joints and marrow, and is a discerner of the thoughts and intents of the heart." **Hebrews 4:12**

The Proverbs 31 woman reaches for the right weapon every time a battle presents itself. It is to her advantage, and it is a privilege to partner with God to protect her mind and that of her loved ones. She arms herself with the God's Word and depends on His promises to renew her mind and protect her heart. Using the right weapons in this great battle ensures living a life of victory.

"Do not conform to the pattern of this world, but be transformed by the renewing of your mind. Then you will be able to test and approve what God's will is—his good, pleasing and perfect will." **Romans 12:2 NIV**

Faith in Application

1. Take negative thoughts captive by replacing it with God's Word. For example, if you feel afraid, pray "I am not fearful for

the Lord has not given me a spirit of fear but power, love and a sound mind."

2. Taking thoughts captive takes practice, but with repetition comes greater authority and ease. Do not allow the enemy to run your thought life. He has power, but you have authority over him!

3. Renew your mind daily in the Bible. Use a concordance or Google to locate scriptures related with your challenges or areas in which you are developing. Write the scriptures and post them throughout your home, car or workplace to remind yourself of the Lord's promises and your spiritual identity.

Questions to Ponder

1. How can you ensure your mind remains aligned with the Word of God rather than entertaining carnality?

2. Our eyes and ears are portholes to our soul. If you truly want to master your thought life, you must become serious of what enters the mind through those senses. Be careful of song lyrics, television shows, YouTube videos, and movies. Choose the kind of entertainment that educates and edifies.

Day 13, Chapter 13
Physical Power

"She equips herself with strength [spiritual, mental, and physical
fitness for her God-given task] and makes her arms strong."
Proverbs 31:17 AMP

T he physical health of the Proverbs 31 woman is as important as her mental health. She keeps her inward home well,
fueling her body with the best nutrition, exercise, and
rest, so that she is able to complete the race.

"Christ is the visible image of the invisible God. He existed
before anything was created and is supreme over all creation, for
through him God created everything in the heavenly realms and
on earth. He made the things we can see and the things we can't
see — such as thrones, kingdoms, rulers, and authorities in the
unseen world. Everything was created through him and for him."
Colossians 1:15-16 NLT

If everything was created for and by God, the way we care for
our bodies should mimic the worship we have for Him. What we

consume - physically or mentally - either defends or questions our faith in Jesus Christ.

The Proverbs 31 woman refrains from being impacted by a culture of self-indulgence, gluttony, and lack of discipline, but instead embraces wisdom about what enters the body and the exercise in which it participates in. She engages in periods of feasting and fasting, equipping her body for earthly duties and her spiritual walk.

"But He answered and said, "It is written, 'Man shall not live by bread alone, but by every word that proceeds from the mouth of God.'" **Matthew 4:4**

When the mind is constantly renewed by the Word, it is easier to make good decisions about healthy nutrition, regular exercise, and adequate sleep. Diets and fitness routines should never be implemented independent of the Word of God. Apart from the Word, they are lifeless, vanity centered, unsustainable, and catering to the trends of the world.

Unless a lifestyle change is rooted in the Word, it will be short-lived and unsuccessful. God informs us that our body is a temple for the Holy Spirit. When we understand the importance of this, we should feel compelled to treat it with greater respect and holy worship.

"Now this I do for the gospel's sake, that I may be partaker of it with you. Do you not know that those who run in a race all run, but one receives the prize? Run in such a way that you may obtain it." **1 Corinthians 9:23-24**

Faith in Application

1. Embrace the "why" for good health. Remind yourself daily that you are to take care of your body well because Christ's

spirit lives within. Post your "why" in your room, car, or any-where you often look. Write your exercise and rest time in your calendar just as you would plan any other activity. Phone apps and reminders can help staying on track.

3. Don't feel pressured to purchase a food delivery program, gym membership or expensive exercise equipment. YouTube videos such as Fitness Blender, Body Rock or Jessica Smith TV are free and can all be completed from home.

Questions to Ponder

1. Examine your lifestyle and decide what drives it. Is it rooted in the Word? Are you seeking God's or man's approval for your choices?

2. What steps can you exercise to honor God with your choices?

Day 14, Chapter 14
Worship & Reflection

Y ou are approaching the halfway mark of this devotional! The spirit of the Lord is always available to you, and He desires that you to enjoy and experience His fullness and grow mightily in the remaining 17 days!

Take time to rest in the Word of God. Reread Proverbs 1-14, and then review the devotions for each day. You might focus, even a second time, on the devotions and scriptures that resonate most with your heart and life space. Be open to encouragement and correction from the Lord.

Remember to answer the questions associated with each devotion. Your thoughts and transparency in writing is key to growth and connection as you walk with the Lord.

Faith in Application

1. Share what you are learning with friends or loved ones. Teaching someone else what you have learned solidifies it for yourself and blesses others.

2. Practice being transparent with others. You may be apprehensive initially to be "real" in a world that wants to wear the perfect image to others. The truth is no one escapes hardship, pain and failure, and when we are courageous enough to be honest with others, they are willing to be real with us, and we no longer feel alone and isolated.

Questions to Ponder

1. Worship songs are powerful. They are an avenue for expressing our love to the Lord, and they prepare our hearts for connection to Him. They also give us instruction and solace when things are hard, and they are the vehicle for expressing joy and gratitude. What are your favorite worship songs to listen to during your quiet time? Make a list of those that are most meaningful in your life and consider why.

2. If you do not have one already, create a morning routine that transitions you into your quiet time. Some like to grab a cup of coffee and dive into reading their Bible. Some begin with worship songs and prayer. Praying the Psalms back to God is an effective way to connect to Him before beginning to study. Some people read devotions and listen to sermons by other pastors. The important thing is that you are consistent about meeting with the Lord every day, preferably in the morning, so it sets the tone and direction for the day.

Day 15, Chapter 15
Self-Examination

"She sees that her gain is good; her lamp does not
go out, but it burns continually through the night
[she is prepared for whatever lies ahead]."
Proverbs 31:18 AMP

The Proverbs 31 woman performs lifelong self-examination to ensure she is not only a hearer but a doer of God's Word. She understands that her spiritual, mental, and physical gains have eternal weight and significance. As such, she is watchful of her actions, thoughts, and behaviors ensuring that she is well prepared, both spiritually and naturally.

"But let each one examine his own work, and then he will have rejoicing in himself alone, and not in another." **Galatians 6:4**

"for not the hearers of the law are just in the sight of God, but the doers of the law will be justified;" **Romans 2:13**

The overall goal of self-examination is to identify strongholds and make corrections as one is convicted by the truth. This continual process of reflection calls for humility, surrendering false beliefs, riches, and status to ultimately grow in one's divine calling.

"Then Jesus said to His disciples, "If anyone desires to come after Me, let him deny himself, and take up his cross, and follow Me." **Matthew 16:24**

Self-reliance and self-determination hinder growth in the Spirit. When we trust in and rely on God's love, grace and mercy instead, problems with pride dissipate and God can complete the work in us to make us whole and holy. Our job is to participate in the process of sanctification as God instructs and leads.

"My sheep hear my voice, and I know them, and they follow me. And I give them eternal life, and they shall never perish; neither shall anyone snatch them out of my hand." **John 10:27-28**

The Proverbs 31 woman's continued acceptance and application of the truth enables her light to shine bright, equipping her to be prepared for whatever lies ahead. Nothing catches her off guard, as she and the Spirit of the Lord are in eternal sync.

The faith walk with Christ is a lifelong journey. Excellent women keep moving forward in the process of sanctification that daily makes us more like our Lord.

Faith in Application

1. Periodically perform a self-evaluation of your spirit life. Sit with the Lord and list the priorities on which He desires you to focus for spiritual growth. Use the questions below as a guide. Refer back to your responses often to ensure you are growing and not remaining stagnant.

2. Receive counsel from a trusted spiritual advisor such as a Pastor or mentor for accountability.

Questions to Ponder

1. Do your relationships, conduct, character, and conversations reflect Christ and influence others to pursue Christ for their own lives?

2. Are there any areas you need to fully surrender to the Lord in order to be a true doer of the word?

3. In what areas do you need to mature to reap spiritual and earthy benefits?

4. Are you doing anything solely for the praise of others?

Day 16, Chapter 16
Willing Hands

"She stretches out her hands to the distaff,
and her hand holds the spindle."
Proverbs 31:19

The Proverbs 31 woman understands that willing hands result in various forms of wealth for her home and loved ones. She discerns her family's needs and is resourceful in obtaining them. She is not intimidated by the type or amount of work required.

"He who has a slack hand becomes poor, but the hand of the diligent makes rich." **Proverbs 10:4**

Her industrious nature and God-given strength fuel the creativity and energy required to complete tasks with efficiency, cheer and diligence. By heeding the voice of the Lord, she is wiser regarding decisions she makes about her home and family, including whether she should work outside the home to supplement the household's income.

"The hand of the diligent will rule, but the lazy man will be put to forced labor." **Proverbs 12:24**

While rest has its place, the Proverbs 31 woman is not lazy. The spirit of slothfulness has no place in her life. She constantly scans her home for spiritual and physical growth, and always seeks to make room for improvements.

"The wise woman builds her house, but the foolish one pulls it down with her hands." **Proverbs 14:1**

As "excellent women", we have the honor of using our hands to build our home equity. Even routine tasks, including laundering, cooking, and cleaning invite comfort and stability in the household and transfer love and care to its members. Whether working inside the home exclusively or outside of the home as well, the Proverbs 31 woman skillfully uses her hands to edify her home for the glory of God.

Faith in Application

1. Examine your home for areas of improvement. Are you constantly behind on laundry or other chores? Research the best system that will work for you. Try completing chores that can easily pile up such as laundry and dishes in small batches every day.

2. If you work outside of the home, plan the completion of your household chores prior to leaving the home for the day, especially what you will serve for dinner that evening. This ensures that when you arrive home after a long day, dinner is near ready.

Questions to Ponder

1. How do you ensure you operate from a spirit of willingness vs slothfulness as you build your home?

2. What plan do you need to put in place to attend to the needs of your household so that you create an environment that is orderly, calm and lovely?

Day 17, Chapter 17
Community & Friendship

"She extends her hand to the poor; yes, she
reaches out her hands to the needy."
Proverbs 31:20

The Proverbs 31 woman has a hospitable spirit and enjoys tending to the spiritual and physical needs of her community. She offers words of kindness and compassion, counsel when sought, and help whenever needed. God calls us to serve others in need. It brings glory to Him and is one component of the purpose for which He has designed us. Helping others in need results in clearer perspective about our own lives and is a powerful antidote for selfishness and self-pity.

Being an excellent friend is also important to the Proverbs 31 woman. She is intentional about giving of herself to her friends—her time, words of affirmation and solace, and support in various forms.

"The heartfelt counsel of a friend is as sweet as perfume and incense." **Proverbs 27:9 NLT**

"As iron sharpens iron, so a man sharpens the countenance of his friend." **Proverbs 27:17**

She edifies her friends and fiercely protects them, the relationship and their fellowship. She refuses to gossip, engage in destructive conversation, or allow for envy. She is careful not to be overly sensitive or prone to hurt or insult. She is intentional about focusing on the positive and breathing life into her friendships in which she encourages a focus on faith rather than the world.

"Let no corrupt word proceed out of your mouth, but what is good for necessary edification, that it may impart grace to the hearers." **Ephesians 4:29**

"He who walks with wise men will be wise, but the companion of fools will be destroyed." **Proverbs 13:20**

Daily communion with the Lord, prayer, and fellowship with like-minded believers results in discernment and strength for the Proverbs 31 woman who is enabled to be a loyal friend, an effective helper, and a powerful resource to others.

Faith in Application

1. Examine your close friendships. Inner circle friends should encourage your pursuit of Christ, offer wise counsel based on the Lord's Word, tell you the truth in love when you are wrong, and hold you accountable to your goals. This circle of friends is typically limited to 1-3 people. These people have your best interest at heart and love you without expectation and unconditionally. Do you have such a circle? If not, create such a group by being this kind of friend first.

2. Examine your outer circle friendships. These are important

but may not serve you in the same way as your close friends. Relationships can be fluid and flexible, and can operate on different levels in your life depending on the other person's faith walk and maturity. Use discernment about when and how much of your heart and trust to share and invest.

Questions to Ponder

1. How can you ensure you are surrounded by spirit filled relationships that reflect the Word of God?

2. How can you better meet the needs of your community?

3. What steps can you take to be willing and available to help others?

Day 18, Chapter 18
Preparedness

"She does not fear the snow for her household,
for all in her household are clothed in [expensive] scarlet [wool]."
Proverbs 31:21 AMP

The Proverbs 31 woman's solid relationship with the Lord strengthens her for a fearless journey, preparing her for what lies ahead. She handles her husband's work/business obligations and appointments, children's school projects and events, and their personal commitments and affairs well. She fulfills wisely these responsibilities, and is ready with what her family members need.

Anticipating needs and future oriented planning is a part of wise stewardship. For example, she doesn't wait until her child has outgrown his shoes and is at the mercy of a full purchase buy; she bought the next size on sale and tucked it away in a storage bin with his next clothing size. The Proverbs 31 woman is the type of shopper who buys the households' new coats during the winter clearance sale when everyone else is shopping for summer.

She ensures not only the best price but also the best quality and tastefulness. She wants her family to look their best for the lowest cost possible.

The foolish or unprepared woman lives at the mercy of the market. She does not create and live within a budget or plan ahead to take advantage of discounts. She waits until the last minute to solve problems and, as a result, does not resolve issues as wisely as possible. The consequence is chaos, discontent and failure. Instead of a life and home of calm and joy, all becomes overwhelming and irritating, and she fails at providing predictability and security for her family members.

God expects us to be wise stewards of all with which He has entrusted us. We glorify Him when we exercise responsibility and wise judgment.

"Even though I walk through the darkest valley, I will fear no evil, for you are with me; your rod and your staff, they comfort me." **Psalm 23:4 NIV**

"A prudent person foresees danger and takes precautions. The simpleton goes blindly on and suffers the consequences." **Proverbs 27:12 NLT**

Faith in Application

1. Write down the family's obligations on a calendar. iCal and Google calendar are phone apps that allow calendar sharing to ensure multiple calendars can be combined so no event is missed.

2. The quality of clothing and household items in thrift and consignment stores has increased drastically. Many thrift

stores offer an additional discount off purchases on certain days of the week. Online resale stores, including Poshmark.com, offer name brand items for a fraction of the cost. Before shopping at a department store, look for specific items online and at discount stores. The key is to go often.

3. Open an online, high yield savings account (American Express Online Savings or Barclays Online Savings are two types) into which money can be deposited for future purchases. Long term financial planning is critical for a family. Education expenses, vacations, and unexpected big ticket items must be anticipated and saved for, even if, at the beginning, the deposits are modest.

Questions to Ponder

1. How do you ensure your household is prepared for what lies ahead?

2. How can you better plan for items requiring long term budgeting?

Day 19, Chapter 19
Appearance

"She makes a tapestry for herself; her clothing
is fine linen and purple."
Proverbs 31:22

In biblical times, purple, a rare and expensive dye, was often the color worn by royalty. Purple became the symbol for wealth and majesty. Those who wore the color were treated with greater respect. Proverbs tells us that a well-dressed woman with a well-decorated home is a blessing. She appreciates beauty, and works to create it in her environment and to maintain it in her appearance, so that she is a blessing to her husband and children.

The Proverbs 31 woman does not neglect her physical appearance, but allocates time daily to look her best. She dresses modestly, but as fashionably as her budget allows. She carries herself with dignity and brings honor to her husband and glory to God.

"An excellent wife is the crown of her husband, but she who causes shame is like rottenness in his bones." **Proverbs 12:4**

A nicely decorated and cared for home is also important. As the CEO of her home, she ensures that her household is functional, tidy and as lovely as possible. It should be a place where the family feels comfortable and free to invite others. A well-ordered home that is beautiful as well is a blessing for those who live there and for those who visit. It demonstrates self-respect, elicits respect from others, and brings honor to the Lord.

"I will praise You, for I am fearfully and wonderfully made; marvelous are Your works, and that my soul knows very well." **Psalm 139:14**

Faith in Application

1. Make a list of new habits you will institute to look your best? Examples are cleansing and applying moisturizer to your face each evening and giving yourself a facial each week (there are lots of recipes online for homemade exfoliators and moisturizers).

2. Wake up thirty minutes earlier than normal to ensure you have time to dress appropriately and apply make-up for the day. If you don't use lipstick, blush or mascara yet before you leave the house, begin adding at least one of them to your routine. They will make a huge difference in how you will feel about yourself when you look in the mirror. YouTube tutorial channels teach how to apply make-up for a polished look.

3. Discard clothing that does not honor God. Ask the Holy Spirit for direction about what to wear that is respectful and modest.

4. Make a To-Do list of changes you will make in your home to improve its appearance and functionality. Then complete one task per week. Use Pinterest to collect home decor ideas. The key is to decorate one room before moving to the next to

focus your design inspiration and not get overwhelmed.

Questions to Ponder

1. What keeps you from getting organized? What can do about the problem?

2. What is your first step in improving your lifestyle?

Day 20, Chapter 20
Her Husband

"Her husband is known in the gates, when he
sits among the elders of the land."
Proverbs 31:23

The husband of the Proverbs 31 woman is a confident leader. He is able to sit peacefully among other men as he knows that his family life is well managed by his wife. He does not question whether his home and children are well cared for, or if their obligations and finances are in order as he has learned to trust and depend on his wife and helpmate completely. This enables him to handle the roles and responsibilities of the Lord's calling on his life well.

"He who finds a wife finds a good thing, and obtains favor from the LORD." **Proverbs 18:22**

The Proverbs 31 woman is the greatest motivator and best cheerleader to the people in her household. As her identity and intentions are rooted in Christ, she selflessly encourages her husband and children with pure motives.

"An excellent wife is the crown of her husband, but she who causes shame is like rottenness in his bones." **Proverbs 12:4**

Her husband therefore not only has a wife but also a true purpose partner. Everything they do is unified, holy and in-sync with God. The Proverbs 31 woman acts as her husband's peripheral vision ensuring that when he discerns a shift from God, she and the household shift with him, guaranteeing a successful outcome. As an "excellent woman", a wife has the honor of being a true life partner with her husband. With her support, encouragement, and respect, they can, as a couple, grab hold of God's vision for the household with strength and purpose.

"Though one may be overpowered by another, two can withstand him. And a threefold cord is not quickly broken." **Ecclesiastes 4:12**

The key for a "virtuous wife" who loves and believes the Lord's instruction that her husband is to be the leader in their household, is to refrain from pressure and nagging and turn to prayer for areas for growth.

Remembering that God calls the husband to love his wife and children as Jesus loves the church, placing their needs and desires first before his own, the wife can trust her husband to choose wisely for the family's well-being so long as He is submitted to the Lord. Wives, that is the prayer for your husband...that he be submitted to the Lord, and that he behave as more and more like Christ, the call for us all.

Faith in Application

1. You are your husband's greatest cheerleader. Husbands gravitate to the sweet voice of encouragement and support

from their wives. Whether it's a promotion at work or just cutting the grass, reward his efforts with words of confirmation and approval. Focusing on the positive and taking time to communicate words of praise is soothing to his soul.

2. Pray regularly for his wise leadership in your home, fulfilling his role in the family as God ordained it, and his ever improving service to the family as he grows in Christ.

Questions to Ponder

1. If married, what more can you do to support your husband so he can confidently pursue his God given purpose?

2. If single, how can you apply these truths to the relationships in your life now and in preparing to be a virtuous wife?

Day 21, Chapter 21
The Word & Reflection

"Charm is deceitful and beauty is passing,
but a woman who fears the Lord, she shall be praised."
Proverbs 31:30

The character, values and behavior of the Proverbs 31 woman should be apparent by now. She is a child of God, a dedicated wife, mother and daughter, a loyal friend and an inspiration and role model in her church and community. She fulfills her responsibilities unto the Lord. She seeks to please Him first and in doing so pleases those around her. She betters the lives of her loved ones in this process by living intentionally, respectfully and responsibly.

As we approach the final leg of this devotion and 31 day challenge, remain disciplined in your *Bible* reading. The daily devotions are a great way to begin your quiet time, however the Word of God activates and sustains long term revelation and change. Be sure to reread Proverbs 1-21 and review the past 20 days of devotions. Focus on the devotions and scriptures that resonate most in your heart and be open to correction and encouragement from the Lord.

"For the word of God is living and powerful, and sharper than any two-edged sword, piercing even to the division of soul and spirit, and of joints and marrow, and is a discerner of the thoughts and intents of the heart." **Hebrews 4:12**

Faith in Application

1. Do you seek a change for you or one of your loved ones? Read and apply the Word through prayer. Confess sin, invite the presence of the Lord, and read certain scriptures over everyone in your household and watch change result.

2. Refer to the blog post titled **'Praying Over Your Children'** at **www.chrystalbernard.com** about how you can cover and protect your family by using the Word of God. I have seen affirmations come to life in the lives of my children and husband as a result of my prayers over them. Believe in the power of the Word and the power of the Lord, and the power of your prayers.

Questions to Ponder

1. How do you handle it when your prayers are not immediately answered? What strategies can you use to persevere knowing that the Lord has your good and His glory in mind always?

2. What changes have you made in your behavior and choices, thus far? List them in your journal and what you have noticed regarding the results.

Day 22, Chapter 22
Creativity & Entrepreneurship

"She makes linen garments and sells them, and supplies
sashes for the merchants."
Proverbs 31:24

G od created the heavens and earth and mankind in His image, so the Proverbs 31 woman understands that God gifted her with the power to be creative too. It is her job to discover how He gifted her and to use those gifts to benefit others. She is driven to fulfill God's purpose for her life, in all its many facets, and to bring glory to Him in fulfilling that purpose.

"Then God said, "Let Us make man in Our image, according to Our likeness; let them have dominion over the fish of the sea, over the birds of the air, and over the cattle, over all the earth and over every creeping thing that creeps on the earth." So God created man in His own image; in the image of God He created him; male and female He created them." **Genesis 1:26-27**

As an entrepreneur at heart, she does not limit business pursuits solely to her experience or educational background. In an effort to pursue God's purpose for her life, she is willing to try new things to determine her interests and talents, and uses wisdom to determine the most sustainable and profitable ideas that will supplement her family's income and benefit her community.

The Lord has gifted us in numerous ways and instilled in us the power to accomplish goals. Unmoved by fear, paralyzing one to stay stagnant, we are to take advantage of the resources God planted within us to bring Him glory. Being called to operate in faith not fear, God enables us to experiment and explore the many avenues afforded to women living in a tech savy age that has simplified getting goods and services to a large audience of consumers.

"For God has not given us a spirit of fear, but of power and of love and of a sound mind." **II Timothy 1:7**

"Then the Lord answered me and said: "Write the vision and make *it* plain on tablets, that he may run who reads it. For the vision *is* yet for an appointed time; But at the end it will speak, and it will not lie. Though it tarries, wait for it; because it will surely come, it will not tarry." **Habakkuk 2:2-3**

Faith in Application

1. Has God given you a business idea to bring to life? Grab your phone or journal and write down the idea and connecting pieces for it to come into reality. Post large sticky notes on your wall so you are constantly reminded of your business concept. Ideas that solely remain in your mind or imagination and are never acted upon remain dreams that never come to be.

2. Fear of the unknown can be paralyzing, but remember the Proverbs 31 woman "laughs at the fear of the future". Fear is a real emotion, but don't give into it. Trust God instead. If God

gave you an idea, He will sustain you through the building stages. The Lord is your main business partner and resource. Go to Him for the next step into a new journey.

3. Expand your network of entrepreneurs in your field of interest. Most entrepreneurs will gladly share their journey about how they started and the keys to success. In the book, "The Millionaire Real Estate Agent", author Gary Keller explains why it is important not to reinvent the wheel, but instead to follow the blueprint of someone who is successful. After business launch, new ideas and unique tweaks can be added.

Questions to Ponder

1. How can you faithfully pursue entrepreneurial endeavors without fear?

2. It's a myth that creativity only lies in the field of arts and entertainment. On what scriptures can you meditate to remind yourself about your God-given creativity and spiritual identity no matter what field you are called to?

3. Speak life over yourself. Repeat the following affirmations:

"God made me in His image. I have His power
to be and do so much more."

"My education and experience do not
limit my dreams and pursuits."

"Faith and trust are my currency."

"Faith trumps fear. God will lead me and guide me."

Day 23, Chapter 23
Fearless

"Strength and honor are her clothing; she shall rejoice
in time to come."
Proverbs 31:25

The Proverbs 31 woman's confidence come from faith and trust in the Lord to shield her and protect her from harm. She knows if she obeys the Lord's commands and is in His will and not her own, she can soar, even in unchartered waters. Faith in His unconditional love for her strengthens and propels her forward with poise and purpose. The volatility and callousness of the world does not thwart her faith in the Lord's promise that "all things will work together for her good and for those who are called according to His purpose".

"The Lord is my strength and my shield; my heart trusted in Him, and I am helped; therefore my heart greatly rejoices, and with my song, I will praise Him." **Psalm 28:7**

"There is no fear in love; but perfect love casts out fear, because fear involves torment. But he who fears has not been made perfect in love." **1 John 4:18**

The Proverbs 31 woman is like a watchman constantly on guard. She harkens to the Lord's voice before considering advice from other sources including self-help books and even counsel from loved ones. She seeks out the Lord to give her words that are affirming, truthful and encouraging to loved ones, friends and colleagues.

The old age saying "Happy Wife, Happy Life" or "If mama's not happy, no one is." speak to the power of the woman in her household. Her attitudes and behaviors set the tone for everyone in the family. Knowing her behavior speaks more powerfully than her words, she is careful about her disposition, demeanor and tone of voice. The Proverbs 31 woman is powerful in creating a loving home with family members who are calm, confident, and courageous. Her strength in the Lord strengthens them.

"Now it shall come to pass, if you diligently obey the voice of the Lord your God, to observe carefully all His commandments which I command you today, and that the Lord your God will set you high above all nations of the earth. And all these blessings shall come upon you and overtake you, because you obey the voice of the Lord your God:" **Deuteronomy 28:1-2**

As "excellent women", we have a choice to walk in fear or joy that comes from faith in the Father's promises and unchanging character. When we walk in strength, so will our loved ones.

Faith in Application

1. Starting the day in prayer and devotion to God shifts your attitude and tone to one more like Christ. Releasing your frustration and worry to the Lord will prevent you from unleashing negative emotions on your loved ones.

2. Before you get out of bed, ask the Holy Spirit to lead and guide you through your day. Pray for His strength through the day, and note the difference in how your day goes when you are depending on him and not yourself.

Questions to Ponder

1. Knowing the impact of your modeling, what steps will you take to guard your words and behavior?

2. How can you know that your decisions are faith based and not influenced by a harsh, unpredictable world?

Day 24, Chapter 24
Wise Words

"She opens her mouth with wisdom, and on
her tongue is the law of kindness."
Proverbs 31:26

Using words as God intended, coupled with our faith, can move mountains. As God's image bearers, believers can call on the same power and authority which spoke the heavens and earth into being. The words we speak therefore are active, alive and powerful. They can create, enhance, and elevate or hurt and destroy. We must be in God's Word daily to ensure that our tongue is aligned with the Spirit of God. Words not directed by the Spirit are lifeless, limiting and lethal.

"Death and life *are* in the power of the tongue, and those who love it will eat its fruit." **Proverbs 18:21**

Words spoken outside of God's direction and wisdom can cause extreme hardship and terrible damage to relationships. Do your words reflect Christ or have they been influenced by a world ruled by Satan who wants to harm us and those we love? Why give the enemy an advantage when you can control your words.

Is your child misbehaving? Examine your words. Remember their tender heart and that they are learning. Has your husband forgotten something? Examine your words. Remember his role, problems, and pressures.

Are your finances in shambles? Examine with your words. Focus not on blame but on fixing the problem. Are you exhausted? Examine your words. Take a power nap before tackling the next chore or issue.

"Be sober, be vigilant; because your adversary the devil walks about like a roaring lion, seeking whom he may devour." **1 Peter 5:8**

If, for whatever reason, you are unable to speak words that are life affirming, do not speak at all until you seek the Lord and pray for His words, not yours. Reread scripture that addresses the power of the tongue. Even King David prayed in Psalm 141 for the Lord to "set a guard over my mouth and keep watch over the door of my lips."

The Proverbs 31 woman partners with the Lord to choose words that are filled with love, grace, and wisdom. It is through her words that Christ is revealed.

Words and Children

Because we live in a fallen world, our children are in the company of both believers and non-believers. In school and at secular functions, they are exposed to ideas and messages that are far from biblical. Parents desire to protect their children from these negative and false notions, but that is not always possible, so it is important that parents begin early with training their children in the way of the Lord and to arm them with God's truth, so they are not confused or led astray by lies.

Praying daily for their protection from evil, for their strength against the forces of evil, and for their willingness to pursue God's purpose for their lives is a tool God has given us. Children need to know that they are a child of the Lord, that the Lord loves them unconditionally, is always present with them, and that His promises are true.

Parents are in covenant relationship with their children, meaning they have a direct responsibility for their children's growth and protection. Teaching children their spiritual identity and Biblical truth is of the utmost importance, so they can disagree with any word spoken over or toward them that is contrary to the Word of God.

Knowing the covenant principles should drive parental behavior, speech and tone to match the grace, mercy and love of the Father. Our words are powerful and can help to anchor the next generation of people's true identity, beliefs, faith and hope in Jesus Christ.

"Let no corrupt word proceed out of your mouth, but what is good for necessary edification, that it may impart grace to the hearers." **Ephesians 4:29**

Faith in Application

1. Practice speaking life giving words. Compliment random people in passing and intentionally applaud those in celebration of an accomplishment. The more you are intentional about speaking life, the easier it will become.

2. If you don't have any life giving words to say, don't speak. Staying quiet is a great strength.

3. For those with children, teach your children the difference between negative and positive words and ideas. Ask them

which words or statements they should accept or reject. This teaches them how to protect their minds and hearts from hurt and harm. This is also a great time to teach scripture to counteract negativity they may encounter.

Questions to Ponder

1. Do your words bring life or harm to the people around you? If you feel convicted, repent and ask for forgiveness from God and from the people you hurt. Don't allow pride to get in the way. Forgiveness is a critical first step for healing and restoration.

2. Are you living out negative words that have been spoken over you? Did someone tell you that you were stupid, or ugly or worthless when you were a child? Did you believe this on any level? Seek out the Lord for healing and the power to forgive that person. Replace those lies with God's truth that you are perfect in His sight, that you have great value, and a mighty purpose.

Day 25, Chapter 25
Priority & Idleness

"She watches over the ways of her household,
and does not eat the bread of idleness."
Proverbs 31:27

The Proverbs 31 woman completes the Lord's plans for her life with a sense of urgency. She understands making reading and obeying the Word a priority in her life as it strengthens her to operate in confidence and intentionality.

Remaining spiritually idle will impact negatively our sanctification process and fulfilling God's purpose for our lives. Slothfulness is one cause of not making the things of God a priority. Life experiences and generational habits can be the cause of slothfulness, and it must be guarded against and actively combated.

"The soul of a lazy man desires, and has nothing; But the soul of the diligent shall be made rich." **Proverbs 13:4**

Are you moving forward or stagnated in your walk with the Lord? The root of inaction (fear, anxiety, and laziness) must be identified and responsibility accepted for change to occur. Ask the Lord to help you keep your focus on Him. Pray for strength and single mindedness so you can look at your schedule and simplify, and/or look at your leisure activities and see where you are wasting your time and energy rather than doing what is the most important activity—your journey with your Lord.

The Proverbs 31 woman rests in the provision and protection of the Lord, enabling her to be on active watch for her household. She understands that when focused on Him, everything aligns. She is not burdened as she has made the one who carries it all, her main priority. The Lord invites us into perfect fellowship, but we have to intentionally make Him the priority.

"But seek first the kingdom of God and His righteousness, and all these things shall be added to you." **Matthew 6:33**

Faith in Application

1. Begin with expressing gratitude each morning before getting out of bed. Express five blessings each morning until the end of the study and note how doing so changed your attitude and even your life. It has been noted that identifying blessings and expressing gratitude actually changes the brain in a positive way.

2. List the ways you may waste time and how to minimize their role in your life.

Questions to Ponder

1. How are you going to make your faith walk a priority?

2. What steps will take to ensure you are going to operate from a place of urgency vs idleness?

Day 26, Chapter 26
The Why

"Her children rise up and call her blessed; her husband
also, and he praises her:"
Proverbs 31:28

W hy make the Lord a priority in your life? Why care for
your body and the Spirit's temple, with exercise and
good nutrition? Why use words that are kind and life
affirming? Why serve others?

Answering the "why" questions about our personal lives re-
quires careful introspection and honest self-analysis. We need to
answer these questions and make changes if we are to be saved for
eternity and experience heaven on earth.

Until our spirit is reconciled with Christ and we accept the
gift of grace and Jesus as our Savior, the soul is linked with ini-
quity (backward thinking), and we are controlled by our flesh. At
the moment of belief in Jesus, we are justified in God's eyes and we
begin the process of sanctification, our deepening walk with the

Lord and the work of becoming more like Christ. If you have not accepted God's gift of salvation, don't risk one more minute and pray the following prayer as no one is promised tomorrow.

Prayer of Salvation

I acknowledge that Jesus Christ is Lord. Forgive me of all sins and living for myself. I invite you to take residence into my life, to teach me your ways and live through me. I make you my Lord and Savior. Amen.

"Watch and pray, lest you enter into temptation. The spirit indeed is willing, but the flesh is weak." **Matthew 26:41**

"For the flesh lusts against the Spirit, and the Spirit against the flesh; and these are contrary to one another, so that you do not do the things that you wish." **Galatians 5:17**

Analyzing and understanding your "whys" will strengthen you to resist the fiery darts of the enemy when he tries to impede the meshing of your soul to the Spirit of the Lord. It will help tame your tongue when it is driven by self-centeredness. It will fortify your faith when questioned and ridiculed. It will anchor you when you step out in faith and trust the Lord with every facet of your life.

As "excellent women", we must profess Christ in all we do and seek to behave more like Him every day. Jesus paid the ultimate price for our salvation. He died so that we would have eternal life with God in heaven. The Proverbs 31 woman is grateful for this unequaled gift, steadfast in her faith, and fully committed to her walk with the Lord, which is also obvious to the others in her life, the reason her husband and children call her blessed and a blessing.

"according to my earnest expectation and hope that in nothing I shall be ashamed, but with all boldness, as always, so now also Christ will be magnified in my body, whether by life or by death. For to me, to live is Christ, and to die is gain." **Philippians 1:20-21**

"looking unto Jesus, the author and finisher of our faith, who for the joy that was set before Him endured the cross, despising the shame, and has sat down at the right hand of the throne of God." **Hebrews 12:2**

Faith in Action

1. Listen to the song 'Nothing Else' by Cody Carnes and pay close attention to the lyrics.

2. Make a list of your whys in your faithful pursuit of Christ. Refer back to the list often especially when your flesh wants to turn to the world.

Questions to Ponder

1. When we accept the gift of salvation, one of our purposes is to live like a follower of Christ and to spread the Gospel to those who do not yet know the Lord. Are you living this calling?

2. If not, how can you better do so?

Day 27, Chapter 27
Authority

"Many daughters have done well, but you excel them all."
Proverbs 31:29

T he *Bible* highlights several women in the *Bible* known for their great works:

Miriam led a nation's women in praise of God (Exodus 15). Deborah, a military advisor, help deliver a nation into the hands of another woman (Judges 4). Queen Esther sacrificed her life for the people of Israel (Esther 4). Hannah was the ideal mother (1 Samuel 1).

These amazing women of the Old Testament loved the Lord and accomplished great acts in His name. How is it possible that a Proverbs 31 woman could possibly be greater than they were? Spiritual authority is not rooted in college degrees or honors, our work or earthly titles, the amount of money we've amassed, or even our bloodline. It is because we have accepted Jesus Christ as our Savior. That makes us a child of the King with the authority of

Jesus, and that makes us no longer subject to the enemy's power. We can resist temptation and say no to sin.

"He has delivered us from the power of darkness and conveyed us into the kingdom of the Son of His love, in whom we have redemption through His blood, the forgiveness of sins." **Colossians 1:13-14**

"even when we were dead in trespasses, He made us alive together with Christ (by grace you have been saved), and raised us up together, and made us sit together in the heavenly places in Christ Jesus, that in the ages to come He might show the exceeding riches of His grace in His kindness toward us in Christ Jesus." **Ephesians 2:5-7**

With faith in Jesus' power and authority, we can declare divine protection over our homes and loved ones, and it will be so. With faith in His power and authority, we can pray boldly and with confidence that the Lord will answer. With faith in His power and authority, we can depend on God's promises.

"So then faith *comes* by hearing, and hearing by the word of God." **Romans 10:17**

"Now faith is the substance of things hoped for, the evidence of things not seen." **Hebrews 11:1**

Christ has given us the keys to the kingdom. Earthy treasures are nothing compared to what is stored up for us in heaven. If we want heaven now, we must pursue Christ, ask for His presence in our life, and in our every minute. Consider Him your greatest friend for His glory and an abiding relationship, crucifying your flesh daily. The Lord wants us free from sin, not solely for our own sake but for the others. It is then we become a powerful testimony, and we defeat the enemy.

"And I will give you the keys of the kingdom of heaven, and

whatever you bind on earth will be bound in heaven, and whatever you loose on earth will be loosed in heaven." **Matthew 16:19**

"Neither give place to the devil." **Ephesians 4:27 KJV**

"The Spirit of the LORD is upon Me, because He has anointed Me to preach the gospel to the poor; He has sent me to heal the brokenhearted, to proclaim liberty to the captives and recovery of sight to the blind, to set at liberty those who are oppressed;" **Luke 4:18**

The Lord has bestowed on us a particular gifting which we are to exercise here on earth. Are you using your gift to share the Gospel and to glorify the Lord? Are you exercising your God-given power and authority to overcome and to flourish? Abide in the Word. Gain strength from the Lord, then tackle your world in a new way.

"Behold, I give you the authority to trample on serpents and scorpions, and over all the power of the enemy, and nothing shall by any means hurt you. Nevertheless do not rejoice in this, that the spirits are subject to you, but rather rejoice because your names are written in heaven." **Luke 10:19-20**

Faith in Application

1. Make a list of scriptures that will remind you of your position and power in Jesus. Refer to it often.

2. Memorize some of those scriptures, so you are armed if the enemy attacks, when you are under pressure, and when you are overwhelmed. Focus on the Lord and exercise His power and peace in every situation.

Questions to Ponder

1. When under pressure do you focus on the Lord or your situations?

2. What will you do in the future when your life feels out of control?

3. What are your spiritual gifts? Determine what they are and make a decision to exercise them and the power Jesus has entrusted to you.

Day 28, Chapter 28
Authority Reflection

"Charm is deceitful and beauty is passing, but a woman
who fears the Lord, she shall be praised."
Proverbs 31:30

As we grow in character and wisdom, we become more confident in our ability to exercise the authority of God's word. God has gifted us with power and purpose. It is our job to exercise both daily as we walk our God ordained paths.

Practice your authority. Write down spiritual areas in which you have been convicted. Speak God's Word over it and expect God's resolution, in His time and in His way. If you see another person struggling, pray for them. Don't settle for saying it in your head or mumbling under your breath. Go to a private space and speak with authority! Cast down any argument the enemy may attempt to raise against your declaration.

Staying strong is a part of the process. The more you exercise your God-given authority, the easier it becomes.

"Therefore submit to God. Resist the devil and he will flee

from you." **James 4:7**

"Behold, I give you the authority to trample on serpents and scorpions, and over all the power of the enemy, and nothing shall by any means hurt you." **Luke 10:19**

Faith in Application

1. If you struggle with knowing what to say to yourself or others, locate scripture about the power of words. (Use Google, a concordance, or this devotional). Then speak the Word over yourself.

Scripture: "A soft answer turns away wrath, but a harsh word stirs up anger." **Proverbs 15:1**

Declare: "Lord help me to respond softly to turn away wrath. I will not use harsh words which stir up anger."

2. Complete this process over and over. By faith you will see the Word begin to work in your life. The key is yielding to the Spirit of the Lord and His word.

Question to Ponder

1. How can you help others to exercise spiritual authority?

Day 29, Chapter 29
Laser Focus

"Charm is deceitful and beauty is passing, but a woman
who fears the LORD, she shall be praised."
Proverbs 31:30

B eing a believer in Christ does not exempt us from trials and
tribulations. We are, in fact, assured that we will suffer in
this world. We will share in Christ's suffering, as well as His
glory.

"These things I have spoken to you, that in Me you may have
peace. In the world, you will have tribulation; but be of good
cheer, I have overcome the world." **John 16:33**

Trials and suffering force us to depend on the Lord for guid-
ance. We must lean into Him, seek His will through His word,
and wait for the wisdom needed to proceed. This combats human
pride, self-autonomy and the desire to control, and builds patience, trust, and faith.

It is through our suffering that we learn empathy for others and selflessness. God uses our suffering to shape us, grow our righteousness, and ultimately reveal our Christlike nature.

"Stand therefore, having girded your waist with truth, having put on the breastplate of righteousness," **Ephesians 6:14**

This is why knowing and applying scripture is crucial to our faith walk. When we look at suffering through this perspective, we can better understand why it is necessary. We humans do not learn best on the mountain tops but the valleys. God promises, however, to be with us always through every moment. He promises no more than we can bear and that there is an eternal reward for our faith and perseverance.

"For our light and momentary troubles are achieving for us an eternal glory that far outweighs them all." **2 Corinthians 4:17 NIV**

"When you pass through the waters, I will be with you; and when you pass through the rivers, they will not sweep over you. When you walk through the fire, you will not be burned; the flames will not set you ablaze." **Isaiah 43:2 NIV**

Studying scripture arms you for battle in the world we can see and the spiritual world we cannot see but are impacted by. One would not enter battle without the right weapons and neither should we try to overcome trials without the correct spiritual armor. Gird yourself with the truth of God's word and stand firm.

Faith in Application

1. Identify the hardest situation you have encountered. Write down the good that has come from it and what you have learned.

2. Write down your testimony. What is your unique story of overcoming tragedy or suffering?

Questions to Ponder

1. How might you better focus on the Lord rather than the situation you are suffering?

2. What is God trying to teach you through a period of suffering?

Day 30, Chapter 30
Fellowship & Sisterhood

"Charm is deceitful and beauty is passing, but a woman
who fears the LORD, she shall be praised."
Proverbs 31:30

T he Lord is faithful in times of joy and sorrow. As He is the beginning and the end of all that there is, He is most aware of the challenges and trials we will face on earth. An omniscient Lord is not surprised by anything, and though He promises to walk with us through the trials, He also admonishes us to join a community of believers who will help, edify, and encourage us.

When we struggle through pain, emotional, spiritual or physical, we often isolate. The Lord wants us to find brethren who will walk hand-in-hand with us, support us through the hard times, and love us as Jesus Christ loves the church.

"Resist him, steadfast in the faith, knowing that the same sufferings are experienced by your brotherhood in the world." **1 Peter 5:9**

"But may the God of all grace, who called us to His eternal glory by Christ Jesus, after you have suffered a while, perfect, establish, strengthen, and settle you." **1 Peter 5:10**

As we have a deep desire to belong, we must seek out people filled with the Holy Spirit in pursuit of Christ. If we do not, we will fill that need with groups, activities, and addictions that satisfy the flesh but never the spirit. Fellowship with other believers in times of joy and trial strengthens us, teaches us, and encourages us.

"And let us consider one another in order to stir up love and good works, not forsaking the assembling of ourselves together, as is the manner of some, but exhorting one another, and so much the more as you see the Day approaching." **Hebrews 10:24-25**

Have you ever traveled outside your native, local country and visited your country's foreign embassy? The community of believer's of Christ is much like a foreign embassy, providing comfort, shelter, and security in times of trouble. In this same manner living in the world but not of the world, the Lord has provided an embassy of His believers for fellowship, prayer, and counsel. As such, a believer is never alone with the vertical relationship of the Lord coupled with the horizontal edification of the brethren. This is true brotherhood and sisterhood.

"A friend loves at all times, and a brother is born for adversity." **Proverbs 17:17**

"As iron sharpens iron, so a man sharpens the countenance of his friend." **Proverbs 27:17**

Faith in Application

1. Join a church's small group or local women's group with like-minded individuals. The key in locating the perfect group

of fellowship is to ensure the group is edifying each member toward Christlike behavior and character.

2. Donate clothes or toys to a local mission, volunteer at a free clinic or your church, or financially support a missionary or a child in need. The best way not to focus on our own troubles is to help other people through theirs.

3. Join the Facebook Proverbs 31 Woman Club with Chrystal Bernard for virtual Holy Spirit-led fellowship. Google search **'Proverbs 31 Woman Club Public Group Facebook'** and join in!

Questions to Ponder

1. Do you belong to a healthy church, small group or sisterly fellowship? If yes, what gifts can you bring to the group to edify others?

2. If not, locate and join a group of fellowship that honors Christ where you can use your gifts to help others.

Day 31, Chapter 31
Well Done, Daughter

"Give her of the fruit of her hands, and let her
own works praise her in the gates."
Proverbs 31:31

L ike the athlete who wins the gold medal, as believers our goal is to hear "well done good and faithful servant" from the Father. This world is only a temporary resting place, but it is also a testing ground to determine our faithfulness to God and trust in His will. If we have accepted the gift of salvation, one day our spirits will enter heaven, and we will live for eternity with the Lord. At that time, He will review with us how well time was spent on earth furthering the Kingdom of God, and He will reward us with crowns for what was accomplished.

It will be either glorious or disappointing. We would all rather glorious, so continue in your quest to become a Proverbs 31 woman; the woman God has called you to be. As His daughters, we hold the keys to the kingdom and, by faith, we willingly exchange human wisdom for His wisdom.

"But seek first the kingdom of God and His righteousness, and all these things shall be added to you." **Matthew 6:33**

Living from this perspective prevents idolizing careers, money, status, accomplishments, husbands, and even children. The struggle is to become less engrossed in worldly activities and relationships and more engrossed with God; to think less about the world and more about the Kingdom.

As the 31 day challenge closes, ask yourself and answer honestly to the following questions:

Am I in full submission to God's will for my life?
Am I holding onto something God wants removed?
Do I idolize my career, family, or status above God?
What was the last thing the Lord instructed me to do? Am I in pursuit of it?

If you feel a tug from the Lord in a certain area, surrender. You may have to detach yourself from certain relationships, mindsets and items of comfort, but God promises to take care of you.

"Behold, I am with you and will keep you wherever you go, and will bring you back to this land; for I will not leave you until I have done what I have spoken to you." **Genesis 28:15**

The Proverbs woman understands her zeal is derived from the love and respect of the Father and that her purpose is clarified through submission to His will. As "excellent women", our goal is to walk hand-in-hand with our Savior for He alone provides the ultimate quench to our spirit and soul.

"His lord said to him, 'Well done, good and faithful servant; you
were faithful over a few things,
I will make you ruler over many things.
Enter into the joy of your lord."
Matthew 25:21

About the Author

Marriage & Motherhood
Chrystal Bernard is the wife to a fun, loving man named Joshua who loves her and his family! Together have three beautiful children, Joshua Jr., Gabriella, and Londyn.

Ministry & Entrepreneurship
Joshua and Chrystal founded **Believer's Connection** in 2014, a church focused on empowering believers to establish and maintain an intimate relationship with Jesus Christ through community fellowship. Believer's Connection is located in Arlington, Texas.

Chrystal is a Certified Public Accountant and founder of The Smart Accountant, an accounting practice assisting individuals and small business owners with tax preparation, bookkeeping and payroll, and personal financial coaching. You can contact Chrystal at **www.chrystalbernard.com.**

Passion

Chrystal's passion and purpose is to encourage and propel women into the person God created them to be by preaching the Word of God through writing, speaking and YouTube videos.

Made in the USA
Columbia, SC
28 May 2023